MW01292001

Biblical Evidence of Men

Before Adam and Eve:

Genesis Revisited

By

Neil R. Goslin LPC

Neil R Goslin 2009.

All Rights Reserved.

This title is always available at Amazon.com.

This book is dedicated to my Grandfather

In Loving Memory of

Perry Pershing Cress

Father, teacher, muse and most of all friend.

Praise for

Biblical Evidence of Men

Before Adam and Eve:

Genesis Revisited

"A must read for Christians and Scientists alike...it moved me."

Tirzah Adams, Formerly of Doubelday

"A very intriguing book...sure to stir the debate..."

Chris Goslin PhD. Professor of Literacy

"A fascinating and marvelous work..."

Helen Kirby, Former Idaho teacher of the year.

Table Of Contents

About This Book

This short book is largely the combined work of many others, synthesized together to perpetuate the authors vision of one possible truth. The information contained herein has been taken from the Bible, the World Wide Web, and other resources such as Steven Hawking, Joseph Silk, John Taylor, George F.R. Ellis, M. Houdmann, P. Matthews-Rose, Randall Niles and many more.

I am not suggesting that these individuals would agree with the premise herein, they may, in fact, entirely disagree. However, they are individuals whom I esteem to be leaders of their respective fields and that is why they are quoted. It is assumed that they are providing facts and that their work is stellar in each of their given areas.

It is not assumed that they agree with my extrapolation and interpretation of the data presented. This author only assumes that their research and knowledge is exceptional and therefore merits inclusion in this larger debate of the differences between theology and science on the specific issue of whether the Bible states that Adam and Eve were the first humans.

This author believes that facts come from both science and Christianity, at first this may seem unusual to most individuals. The intent of this book is to erase some of those lines of disagreement. It is my belief that by the end of this book it will be clear that science and theology are not necessarily mutually exclusive ideas.

This book is designed for the lay scholar and casual seeker of truth and those who diligently work to uncover the mysteries of who we are and where we come from. I hope you enjoy the book.

Neil R. Goslin, August 4, 2009

Chapter One

The Debate

The battle among Christians and scientists often hinges on the biblical scholars assertions that man has only existed for 6,000 years. This appears to be evidenced by the timeline in the Bible, which goes back 6,000 years to Adam and Eve.

There is clear archaeological evidence all over the world that seems to contradict the Bible on this account. So either Adam and Eve were not the first people, or the Bible is false.

In order to ascertain the truth we must of course consult the source, the Bible itself. Does it really say that Adam and Eve were the first beings created, or have we just let ourselves believe that they were?

I will use nothing but the Bible itself to answer these questions from the theological perspective. I will use other scientific sources to answer scientific and archaeological questions.

So we must begin at the beginning. Genesis. In writing this book I want to present both sides with as little bias as I can. I researched this topic in this same fashion when I made my decision about what I believe the truth to be.

The fact is, the Bible does not say that Adam and Eve were the first people. But we will get into that more later. The Bible also does not say that God acted alone in his creation. In fact, it expressly points out that he did not act alone. These things are plainly written in the Bible and are in fact read on a daily basis but are still overlooked somehow.

The most widely used and accepted version of the Bible is the King James Version. In 1604, King James I of England authorized that a new translation of the Bible into English be started. It was finished in 1611, just 85 years after the first translation of the New Testament into English appeared (Tyndale, 1526). The Authorized Version, or King James Version, quickly became the standard for English-speaking Protestants. Its flowing language and prose rhythm has had a profound influence on the literature of the past 300 years.

Due to it's wide acceptance and availability, that is the version I will use. The first passage reads; *1 In the beginning God created the heaven and the earth.* This is probably the most widely read passage of scripture in existence. The first sentence. Sadly, many people stop there, or simply turn off their brains and stop trying to truly understand what it says after this one line.

This is why people assume God acted entirely alone. Doesn't it say that *God created the heaven and the earth?* So he was alone…right? But it states in Genesis Chapter 1 verse 26 *And God said, Let **us** make man in **our** image, after **our** likeness.* Three very obvious references that he is not alone. Let…us…our…our…

Who these beings are has been speculated upon. One speculation that persists is that of a heavenly mother. Yet it has also been asserted that God loved her so much he did not want her name to be uttered so that none could take her name in vain…so I really don't want to dwell on that issue.

Another possibility is Jesus Christ…the Only Begotten Son of the Father; or more likely…all three of them. But there is no way to know…it is only clear that at the point when he made man…he was not alone.

The debate has raged between Christians and Scientists for years and it appears it will go on unless some broader understanding is reached. Within these pages lies the broader understanding that is needed.

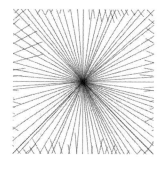

Chapter Two

The First Moments of Creation and The Big Bang

In order to fully appreciate the history of creation we must define who God is. In the Book of Revelation, John describes God as follows.

1After this I looked, and, behold, a door was opened in heaven: and the first voice which I heard was as it were of a trumpet talking with me; which said, Come up hither, and I will shew thee things which must be hereafter.

2And immediately I was in the spirit: and, behold, a throne was set in heaven, and one sat on the throne.

3And he that sat was to look upon like a jasper and a sardine stone: and there was a rainbow round about the throne, in sight like unto an emerald.

4And round about the throne were four and twenty seats: and upon the seats I saw four and twenty elders sitting, clothed in white raiment; and they had on their heads crowns of gold.

5And out of the throne proceeded lightnings and thunderings and voices: and there were seven lamps of fire burning before the throne, which are the seven Spirits of God.

Immediately the mind conjures up images of power and uncertainty, something both glorious and possibly frightening at the same time. It is truly a confusing thing to contemplate. So God is a powerful supernatural being that cannot die and is surrounded by other powerful supernatural beings. This very concept is comforting as well as overwhelming to the human psyche.

The next passages of Genesis are where Christian Theology and science begin to collide. *2And the earth was without form, and void; and darkness was upon the face of the deep. And the Spirit of God moved upon the face of the waters.*

3And God said, Let there be light: and there was light. Scientist refer to this event as "The Big Bang"

The Big Bang theory is an effort to explain what happened at the very beginning of our universe. Discoveries in astronomy and physics have shown beyond a reasonable doubt that our universe did in fact have a beginning. Prior to that moment there was nothing; during and after that moment there was something: our universe. The big bang theory is an effort to explain what happened during and after that moment.

According to the standard theory, our universe sprang into existence as "singularity" around 13.7 billion years ago. What is a "singularity" and where does it come from? Well, to be honest, we don't know for sure. Singularities are zones which defy our current understanding of physics. They are thought to exist at the core of "black holes." Black holes are areas of intense gravitational pressure. The pressure is thought to be so intense that finite matter is actually squished into infinite density (a mathematical concept which truly boggles the mind). These zones of infinite density are called "singularities." Our universe is thought to have begun as an infinitesimally small, infinitely hot, infinitely dense, something - a singularity. Where did it come from? We don't know. Why did it appear? We don't know.

After its initial appearance, it apparently inflated (the "Big Bang"), expanded and cooled, going from very, very small and very, very hot, to the size and temperature of our current universe. It continues to expand and cool to this day and we are inside of it: incredible creatures living on a unique planet, circling a beautiful star clustered together with several hundred billion other stars in a galaxy soaring through the cosmos, all of which is inside of an expanding universe that began as an infinitesimal singularity which appeared out of nowhere for reasons unknown. This is the Big Bang theory.

In a comparison and contrast of the Genesis account of Creation and the explanation of the Big Bang Theory, they are really quite similar. *2And the earth was without form, and void; and darkness was upon the face of the deep. And the Spirit of God moved upon the face of the waters. 3And God said, Let there be light: and there was light.*

When I read the Big Bang Theory the Genesis statement that …*without form, and void; and darkness was upon the face of the deep*…seems to sum it up quite nicely. And then at the moment of the "bang" I can also envision the next statement *3And God said, Let there be light: and there was light.*

So at this point all we know for certain, regardless of whether one chooses to believe in science or religion is that there was an "event".

Chapter Three

The Big Bang Theory Misconceptions

Some common misconceptions to the big bang theory must be noted if we are to be fair.

There are many misconceptions surrounding the Big Bang theory. For example, we tend to imagine a giant explosion. Experts however say that there was no explosion; there was (and continues to be) an expansion. Rather than imagining a balloon popping and releasing its contents, imagine a balloon expanding: an infinitesimally small balloon expanding to the size of our current universe.

Of course this then begs the question, what is this "balloon" expanding into? I don't know the answer but I do know basic laws of physics and of displacement. There certainly is displaced matter when something expands. This matter has to go somewhere.

With a balloon in a room, the balloon expands and according to Boyles Gas Law an amount of gas or air, is displaced or pressurized (if in a sealed container) to accommodate the space needed to allow the balloon to expand.

Yet even if the "Balloon" (known universe) is expanding into a finite space like a room, then the air would become increasingly pressurized. This air would either push back with enough force to create equilibrium or push back harder like ripples of water hitting a barrier and coming back, and the universal expansion would cease or decrease.

This has not happened so we can only assume that the size of the space into which the universe is expanding is so vast as to be beyond human comprehension. This continuing expansion seems to have no intention of stopping.

Big Bang Theorist argue that:

Another misconception is that we tend to image the singularity as a little fireball appearing somewhere in space. According to the many experts however, space didn't exist prior to the Big Bang. Back in the late '60s and early '70s, when men first walked upon the moon, "three British astrophysicists, Steven Hawking, George Ellis, and Roger Penrose turned their attention to the Theory of Relativity and its implications regarding our notions of time. In 1968 and 1970, they published papers in which they extended Einstein's Theory of General Relativity to include measurements of time and space.[1,2] According to their calculations, time and space had a finite beginning that corresponded to the origin of matter and energy."[3] The singularity didn't appear *in* space; rather, space began inside of the singularity. Prior to the singularity, *nothing* existed, not space, time, matter, or energy - nothing. So where and in what did the singularity appear if not in space? We don't know. We don't know where it came from, why it's here, or even where

it is. All we really know is that we are inside of it and at one time it didn't exist and neither did we.

Frankly this argument seems absurd to our human brains yet it strangely supports creation. It is stated that "According to their calculations, time and space had a finite beginning that corresponded to the origin of matter and energy." Compared with *3And God said, Let there be light: and there was light.* It seems to make a pretty good argument for creation.

But in my promise of fairness let me go on.

What are the major evidences that support the Big Bang theory?

- First of all, we are reasonably certain that the universe had a beginning.

- Second, galaxies appear to be moving away from us at speeds proportional to their distance. This is called "Hubble's Law," named after Edwin Hubble (1889-1953) who discovered this phenomenon in 1929. This observation supports the expansion of the universe and suggests that the universe was once compacted.

- Third, if the universe was initially very, very hot as the Big Bang suggests, we should be able to find some remnant of this heat. In 1965, Radioastronomers Arno

Penzias and Robert Wilson discovered a 2.725 degree Kelvin (-454.765 degree Fahrenheit, -270.425 degree Celsius) Cosmic Microwave Background radiation (CMB) which pervades the observable universe. This is thought to be the remnant which scientists were looking for. Penzias and Wilson shared in the 1978 Nobel Prize for Physics for their discovery.

- Finally, the abundance of the "light elements" Hydrogen and Helium found in the observable universe are thought to support the Big Bang model of origins.

Is this science or another way to frame Genesis? *4And God saw the light, that it was good: and God divided the light from the darkness. 5And God called the light Day, and the darkness he called Night. And the evening and the morning were the first day.*

Is the standard Big Bang theory the only model consistent with these evidences? No, it's just the most popular one. Internationally renown Astrophysicist George F. R. Ellis explains: "People need to be aware that there is a range of models that could explain the observations….For instance, I can construct you a spherically symmetrical universe with Earth at its center, and you cannot disprove it based on observations….You can only exclude it on philosophical grounds. In my view there is absolutely nothing wrong in that. What I want to bring into the open is the fact that we are using philosophical criteria in choosing our models. A lot of cosmology tries to hide that."[4]

In 2003, Physicist Robert Gentry proposed an attractive alternative to the standard theory, an alternative which also accounts for the evidences listed above.[5] Dr. Gentry claims that the standard Big Bang model is founded upon a faulty paradigm (the Friedmann-lemaitre expanding-spacetime paradigm) which he claims is inconsistent with the empirical data. He chooses instead to base his model on Einstein's static-spacetime paradigm which he claims is the "genuine cosmic Rosetta." Gentry has published several papers outlining what he considers to be serious flaws in the standard Big Bang model.[6] Other high-profile dissenters include Nobel laureate Dr. Hannes Alfvén, Professor Geoffrey Burbidge, Dr. Halton Arp, and the renowned British astronomer Sir Fred Hoyle, who is accredited with first coining the term "the Big Bang" during a BBC radio broadcast in 1950.

So there is clearly no scientific consensus on the creation of the universe; only a statement that it came from nothing. Unfortunately for the scientific camp this seems to corroborate creation.

Chapter Four

Of God and Science

The Big Bang Theorist themselves ask the question. What about God? Any discussion of the Big Bang theory would be incomplete without asking the question, what about God? This is because cosmogony (the study of the origin of the universe) is an area where science and theology meet. Creation was a supernatural event. That is, it took place outside of the natural realm. This fact begs the question: is there anything else which exists outside of the natural realm? Specifically, is there a master Architect out there? We know that this universe had a beginning. Was God the "First Cause"?

Does God exist? An answer to this fundamental question is a prerequisite for answering the other big questions of life: Where did we come from? Why are we here? Do we serve a purpose? Do we have any intrinsic value? What happens after we die? The question of the existence of God is fundamental.

Before we ask the question "Does God exist?" we first have to deal with our philosophical predispositions. If, for example, someone was already dedicated to the philosophical idea that nothing can exist outside of the natural realm (i.e. there can be no supernatural God), no amount of evidence could convince them otherwise. Asking the question "does God exist?" would be pointless. Their answer would be "No, He doesn't," regardless of whether God truly exists or not.

The question would be impossible to answer from an evidentiary standpoint simply because anything which God might have done (that is, any supernatural act which might serve as evidence for His existence) would have to be explained away in terms of natural causes. This would be so not because we know what those natural causes could possibly be, but simply because a supernatural God is not allowed to exist in the mind of the closed minded thinker.

Dr. Richard Lewontin, the Alexander Agassiz Professor of Zoology at Harvard University, put it like this: "It is not that the methods and institutions of science somehow compel us to accept a material explanation of the phenomenal world, but, on the contrary, that *we are forced by our a priori adherence to material causes* to create an apparatus of investigation and a set of concepts that produce material explanations, no matter how counterintuitive, no matter how mystifying to the uninitiated. Moreover, that materialism is absolute, for *we cannot allow a Divine*

Foot in the door" (Richard Lewontin, "Billions and Billions of Demons," *New York Review of Books,* January 9, 1997, p. 28).

If, on the other hand, this person was neutral, and didn't already have an "a priori adherence" to a particular worldview (be it naturalistic or otherwise), the question "does God really exist?" wouldn't be pointless at all. Rather, it would be the first step in an objective and meaningful search for ultimate truth. Our willingness to ask the question with an open mind is fundamental to our ability to discover the truth behind the answer. So first of all, before you even ask the question, decide whether or not you're really willing to accept the answer.

Once you're ready to ask the question, "does God exist?" here are a few observations to consider as you begin your search for an objective answer:

- Discoveries in astronomy have shown beyond a reasonable doubt that the universe did, in fact, have a beginning. There was a single moment of creation.

- Advances in molecular biology have revealed vast amounts of information encoded in each and every living cell, and molecular biologists have discovered thousands upon thousands of exquisitely designed machines at the molecular level. Information requires intelligence and design requires a designer.

- Biochemists and mathematicians have calculated the odds against life arising from non-life naturally via unintelligent processes. The odds are astronomical. In fact, scientists aren't even sure if life could have evolved naturally via unintelligent processes. If life did not arise by chance, how did it arise?

- The universe is ordered by natural laws. Where did these laws come from and what purpose do they serve?

- Philosophers agree that a transcendent Law Giver is the only plausible explanation for an objective moral standard. So, ask yourself if you believe in right and wrong and then ask yourself why. Who gave you your conscience? Why does it exist?

- People of every race, creed, color, and culture, both men and women, young and old, wise and foolish, from the educated to the ignorant, claim to have personally experienced something of the supernatural. So what are we supposed to do with these prodigious accounts of divine healing, prophetic revelation, answered prayer, and other miraculous phenomena? Ignorance and imagination may have played a part to be sure, but is there something more?

If your curiosity has been piqued and you desire to look into this matter further, I recommend that you consider the world's assortment of so-called Holy Books. If God does exist, has He revealed Himself? And if He has revealed Himself, surely He exists...

Christians clearly believe he has revealed himself.

Chapter Five

Evidence of God

To the Christian population the evidence of the existence of God is found in the Bible. The Holy Bible is a phenomenal account of history, comprised of 66 books, written over approximately 1600 years, by at least 40 distinct authors. The Old Testament (Old Covenant) contains 39 books written from approximately 1500 to 400 BC, and the New Testament (New Covenant) contains 27 books written from approximately 40 to 90 AD. The Jewish Bible (*Tenach*) is the same as the Christian Old Testament, except for its book arrangement. The original Old Testament was written mainly in Hebrew, with some Aramaic, while the original New Testament was written in Greek.

The Holy Bible begins with the Jewish Scriptures. The historical record of the Jews was written down in leather scrolls and tablets over centuries, and the authors included kings, shepherds, prophets and other leaders inspired by God. In Exodus, God tells Moses to write the Law (*Torah*) in a book. About 450 BC, all of the Jewish scriptures were collected and arranged by councils of rabbis, who then recognized the complete set as the inspired and sacred authority of God. Beginning as early as 250 BC, the Hebrew Bible (*Tenach*) was translated into Greek by Jewish scholars in Alexandria, Egypt. The translation became known as the Septuagint, meaning 70, and referring to the tradition that 70 or 72 men comprised the translation team. At this point, the books of the Hebrew Bible were arranged by topic, including history, poetry, and prophecy. In 90 AD, at the Council of Jamnia, the Jewish elders established the final Hebrew Bible canon. Although the Jewish Scriptures were copied by hand, they were extremely accurate copy to copy. The Jews had a phenomenal system of scribes, who developed intricate and ritualistic methods for counting letters, words and paragraphs to insure that no copying errors were made. In fact, scribal tradition was maintained until the invention of the printing press in 1455. As far as manuscript accuracy, the recent discovery of the Dead Sea Scrolls has confirmed the remarkable reliability of the Old Testament texts over the years.

After approximately 400 years of scriptural silence, Jesus arrived on the scene in about 4 BC. Throughout His teaching, Jesus often quotes the Old Testament, declaring that He did not come to destroy the Jewish Scriptures, but to fulfill them.

In Luke 24:44-45, Jesus proclaims to his disciples, "All things must be fulfilled, which were written in the law of Moses, and in the prophets, and in the psalms, concerning me." Starting in about 40 AD and continuing to about 90 AD, the eye-witnesses to the life of Jesus Christ, including Matthew, Mark, Luke, John, Paul, James, Peter and Jude write the Gospels, letters and books that later become the New Testament. These authors quote from 31 books of the Old Testament, and widely circulate their material so that by about 150 AD, early Christians were referring to the set of writings as the New Covenant. During the 200s AD, the writings were translated into Latin, Coptic (Egypt) and Syriac (Syria) and widely disseminated. At this time, at least 21 of the writings were considered canonical. Thereafter, in 397 AD, the current 27 books of the New Testament were formally confirmed and canonized in the Synod of Carthage.

Like the Old Testament, we now have significant evidence that the New Testament we read today is remarkably accurate as compared to the original manuscripts. Of the thousands of copies made by hand before the printing press, we have approximately 24,000 manuscripts, including more than 5,300 Greek manuscripts from the New Testament alone. The Bible is better preserved, by far, than accepted writings of Homer, Plato and Aristotle. Of course, as the Bible was carried from country to country, it was translated into languages that don't necessarily mirror the original languages of Greek and Hebrew. However, other than grammatical and cultural differences, God's Word has been remarkably preserved and translated over the years. The Bible now gives inspiration to hundreds of millions throughout the world – that's because the Christians believe that the Bible is truly the inspired Word of God (2 Timothy 3:16-17 and 2 Peter 1:20-21).

"Who wrote the Bible" is a question that is undoubtedly asked by many who are familiar with the impact this book has made on people around the world. The Bible gives guidance in our journey through life to eternity, as well as leads us to a relationship with the God of the universe. It is a historical book that is backed by archeology, and a prophetic book that has lived up to all of its claims thus far. In light of all these facts, asking, "who wrote the Bible," is a vital question that deserves serious investigation and a serious response. The Bible is God's letter to humanity collected into 66 books written by 40 divinely inspired writers. These writers come from all walks of life (i.e., kings to fishermen) and spans over a period of 1,500 years or more. These claims may seem dramatic (or unrealistic to some), but a careful and honest study of the biblical scriptures will show them to be true.

"Who wrote the Bible" is a question that can be definitively answered by examining the biblical texts in light of the external evidences that supports its claims. 2 Timothy 3:16 states that "All scripture is inspired by God…." In 2 Peter 1:20-21, Peter reminds the reader to "know this first of all, that no prophecy of scripture is a matter of one's own interpretation, … but men moved by the Holy

Spirit spoke from God." The Bible itself tells us that it is God who is the author of His book.

God does not leave us with just claims of His divine handiwork in the Bible, but also supports it with compelling evidence. The design of the Bible itself is a miracle. Written over more than 1,500 years by vastly different writers, yet every book in the Bible is consistent in its message. These 66 books talk about history, prophecy, poetry, and theology. Despite their complexity, differences in writing styles and vast time periods, the books of the Bible agree miraculously well in theme, facts and cross-referencing. No human beings could have planned such an intricate combination of books over a 1,500-year time span. Bible manuscripts (remember, there were no printing presses until 1455) have survived despite weather, persecution and time. Most ancient writings written on weak materials like papyrus have vanished all together. Yet many copies of the Old Testament scriptures survived. For instance, the Dead Sea Scrolls contain all books of the Old Testament, except Esther, and have been dated to before the time of Christ. Consider Julius Caesar's Gallic Wars. Only ten copies written about 1,000 years after the event are in existence. In comparison, there are over 24,000+ New Testament manuscripts, the earliest one dating to within 24 years after Christ. The Bible also validates its divine authorship through fulfilled prophecies. An astonishing 668 prophecies have been fulfilled and none have ever been proven false (three are unconfirmed). An honest study of biblical prophecy will compellingly show the divine authorship of the Bible. Further, archeology confirms (or in some cases supports) accounts in the biblical record. No other holy book comes close to the Bible in the amount of evidence supporting its divine authorship. "Who Wrote the Bible" is indeed a question that everyone must ask. If indeed it is the Word of the living God, then no other book gives us more insight into our lives, more hope for our future, and a true path to a relationship with God. Search the Bible with openness and honesty and see for yourself what the Creator of the universe wants to tell you.

God may not be provable through mathematical formulae or properties of physics, but we live in an era where the evidence of God is all around us. Just look through the Hubble Telescope and peer to the edge of the massive cosmos. View the monitor of an electron-scanning microscope and delve into the intricate world of an organic cell. Sit down and read an entire library of information that reveals the complexity of the digital code that turns a fertilized egg into a human being. Study principles of quantum mechanics and investigate the world of extra-dimensionality. Review the nature of your conscience, subconscious, standards of morality, thoughts of religion. Then, try to reconcile all of these realities with a basic theory of randomness. Not believing in God is much more of a "leap of faith" than ever.

God - A brief summary of the key arguments:

- **Order**. God provides the best explanation for abstract notions, such as numbers, formulas and properties.

- **Causation**. God provides the best explanation for the existence of the universe and all that is in it.

- **Design**. God provides the best explanation for the complex order in cosmological and biological entities.

- **Morality**. God provides the best explanation for the existence of objective moral/ethical values in the world. In Romans 5:12, we read that "sin entered the world through one man, and through sin - death, and thus death has spread through the whole human race because everyone has sinned."

God has been described as everything from an impersonal "life force" to a personal Creator, from Mother Nature to Almighty Lord. While mankind creates various characters for God over time, we should actually look to the timeless standards of truth already delivered in the Bible.

Of course, one must establish the credibility and reliability of the Bible before endeavoring to define God through the Bible. Well, like no time in history, we have established the truth of the Biblical record. Just explore the archaeological treasures that establish the veracity of Biblical events. Review the recently discovered manuscripts, such as the Dead Sea Scrolls, which prove the reliability of the Biblical texts. Study the over 600 fulfilled prophecies contained in Biblical scripture, including the actual fulfillment of prophecy in Israel over the last few decades. Read the Bible itself as an intellectual undertaking and discover the inherent complexity and integration contained in its 66 books, written by 40 inspired authors, over a period of approximately 1,600 years.

God -- Once you've established that the Bible is a credible and reliable document, this is the first place to look for His true character and attributes. As you explore the Bible, you will discover His unchanging nature. God is infinite and eternal. God is sovereign. God is omnipotent (all-powerful), omniscient (all-knowing) and omnipresent (all places at all times). God is perfectly holy and perfectly just. God is wisdom, power, glory, righteousness, mercy, faithfulness, goodness, beauty, and patience. God is love. God is truth.

Chapter Six

The First Man

So far we have established that it is very nearly impossible to discern the facts without either having faith in God or faith in Science. There does not seem to be a clear-cut answer.

So…does the Bible say that Adam is the first man? In fact…it does not. The rest of Genesis Chapter one is as follows.

26And God said, Let us make man in our image, after our likeness: and let them have dominion over the fish of the sea, and over the fowl of the air, and over the cattle, and over all the earth, and over every creeping thing that creepeth upon the earth.

27So God created man in his own image, in the image of God created he him; male and female created he them.

28And God blessed them, and God said unto them, Be fruitful, and multiply, and replenish the earth, and subdue it: and have dominion over the fish of the sea, and over the fowl of the air, and over every living thing that moveth upon the earth.

29And God said, Behold, I have given you every herb bearing seed, which is upon the face of all the earth, and every tree, in the which is the fruit of a tree yielding seed; to you it shall be for meat.

30And to every beast of the earth, and to every fowl of the air, and to every thing that creepeth upon the earth, wherein there is life, I have given every green herb for meat: and it was so.

31And God saw every thing that he had made, and, behold, it was very good. And the evening and the morning were the sixth day.

This is the end of Chapter One of Genesis and Adam has yet to appear. Yet there they are. *26And God said, Let us make man in our image, after our likeness: and let them have dominion over the fish of the sea, and over the fowl of the air, and over the cattle, and over all the earth, and over every creeping thing that creepeth upon the earth.*

27So God created man in his own image, in the image of God created he him; male and female created he them.

28And God blessed them, and God said unto them, Be fruitful, and multiply, and replenish the earth, and subdue it: and have dominion over the fish of the sea, and over the fowl of the air, and over every living thing that moveth upon the earth. And it appears to be a very complete story.

In fact Genesis Chapter 2 goes on to say…*1Thus the heavens and the earth were finished, and all the host of them.*

*2And on the seventh day **God ended his work** which he had made; and he rested on the seventh day from all his work which he had made.*

*3And God blessed the seventh day, and sanctified it: **because that in it he had rested from all his work which God created and made.***

God the father was done. But there is much more evidence in the Bible itself. So where are Adam and Eve? The race of man has been created and we have no idea when. We are not yet up to the very recent time of Adam and Eve.

Not long ago my son and I built a fence. It was mostly me…that's how building with sons often goes. I built the first half entirely by myself. I dug holes two feet deep, I installed posts, I put up rails and panels, and then I took my son and showed him what I had done. Not unlike where God says. *Let us make man in **our** image, after **our** likeness:* That's right, he is not acting alone. He suggests that he had his son with him. He engaged in this endeavor with His oldest son, His *Only Begotten Son.*

Do I have evidence of this? In fact, yes I do.

*4These are the generations of the heavens and of the earth when they were created, in the day that the **LORD God** made the earth and the heavens,*

5And every plant of the field before it was in the earth, and every herb of the field before it grew:

The Lord God is a different entity. Thus far in the book the entity is referred to as God. So why would the Bible say the *Lord God* now? The word "God" in the Hebrew is Elohim. According to Ellis Rasmussen the Lord God is Jehovah Elohim. The meaning of the combination of the two permits a genitive relationship of two nouns thus placed together. Jehovah is Jesus Christ.

So God acts like any one of us might act. He takes his oldest and only begotten son and tells him, "Now you finish it".

It is important to reiterate that ***5And every plant of the field before it was in the earth, and every herb of the field before it grew:*** Jesus was not redoing what was already done. Most people just assume that he is, but he clearly is not.

It goes on to say *for the LORD God had not caused it to rain upon the earth, and there was not a man to till the ground.* This seems to indicate that there was no man at all. That Chapter One never happened.

So does that mean there was no man anywhere? No, it means there was no one in the area that Jesus was creating. Perhaps Eden was a very isolated area. Unpopulated. No one there, not a man to till the ground.

When my son went to finish his part of the fence, there were no holes in the ground, there was not a single fence post up. But my part of the fence was completely done. So from his perspective nothing had been done on what he needed to do. But all of mine was done.

So as he began to work, there was not a place to put a fence post, there was nothing. But behind him, in fact ¾ of the way around the house was done. But his area was untouched, utterly barren.

Let us continue. The evidence will mount.

6But there went up a mist from the earth, and watered the whole face of the ground.

7And the LORD God formed man of the dust of the ground, and breathed into his nostrils the breath of life; and man became a living soul.

8And the LORD God planted a garden eastward in Eden; and there he put the man whom he had formed.

9And out of the ground made the LORD God to grow every tree that is pleasant to the sight, and good for food; the tree of life also in the midst of the garden, and the tree of knowledge of good and evil.

10And a river went out of Eden to water the garden; and from thence it was parted, and became into four heads.

11The name of the first is Pison: that is it which compasseth the whole land of Havilah, where there is gold;

12And the gold of that land is good: there is bdellium and the onyx stone.

13And the name of the second river is Gihon: the same is it that compasseth the whole land of Ethiopia.

14And the name of the third river is Hiddekel: that is it which goeth toward the east of Assyria. And the fourth river is Euphrates.

15And the LORD God took the man, and put him into the garden of Eden to dress it and to keep it.

16And the LORD God commanded the man, saying, Of every tree of the garden thou mayest freely eat:

17But of the tree of the knowledge of good and evil, thou shalt not eat of it: for in the day that thou eatest thereof thou shalt surely die.

18And the LORD God said, It is not good that the man should be alone; I will make him an help meet for him.

19And out of the ground the LORD God formed every beast of the field, and every fowl of the air; and brought them unto Adam to see what he would call them: and whatsoever Adam called every living creature, that was the name thereof.

20And Adam gave names to all cattle, and to the fowl of the air, and to every beast of the field; but for Adam there was not found an help meet for him.

21And the LORD God caused a deep sleep to fall upon Adam, and he slept: and he took one of his ribs, and closed up the flesh instead thereof;

22And the rib, which the LORD God had taken from man, made he a woman, and brought her unto the man.

23And Adam said, This is now bone of my bones, and flesh of my flesh: she shall be called Woman, because she was taken out of Man.

24Therefore shall a man leave his father and his mother, and shall cleave unto his wife: and they shall be one flesh.

25And they were both naked, the man and his wife, and were not ashamed.

Genesis 3

1Now the serpent was more subtil than any beast of the field which the LORD God had made. And he said unto the woman, Yea, hath God said, Ye shall not eat of every tree of the garden?

2And the woman said unto the serpent, We may eat of the fruit of the trees of the garden:

3But of the fruit of the tree which is in the midst of the garden, God hath said, Ye shall not eat of it, neither shall ye touch it, lest ye die.

4And the serpent said unto the woman, Ye shall not surely die:

5For God doth know that in the day ye eat thereof, then your eyes shall be opened, and ye shall be as gods, knowing good and evil.

6And when the woman saw that the tree was good for food, and that it was pleasant to the eyes, and a tree to be desired to make one wise, she took of the fruit thereof, and did eat, and gave also unto her husband with her; and he did eat.

7And the eyes of them both were opened, and they knew that they were naked; and they sewed fig leaves together, and made themselves aprons.

8And they heard the voice of the LORD God walking in the garden in the cool of the day: and Adam and his wife hid themselves from the presence of the LORD God amongst the trees of the garden.

9And the LORD God called unto Adam, and said unto him, Where art thou?

10And he said, I heard thy voice in the garden, and I was afraid, because I was naked; and I hid myself.

11And he said, Who told thee that thou wast naked? Hast thou eaten of the tree, whereof I commanded thee that thou shouldest not eat?

12And the man said, The woman whom thou gavest to be with me, she gave me of the tree, and I did eat.

13And the LORD God said unto the woman, What is this that thou hast done? And the woman said, The serpent beguiled me, and I did eat.

14And the LORD God said unto the serpent, Because thou hast done this, thou art cursed above all cattle, and above every beast of the field; upon thy belly shalt thou go, and dust shalt thou eat all the days of thy life:

15And I will put enmity between thee and the woman, and between thy seed and her seed; it shall bruise thy head, and thou shalt bruise his heel.

16Unto the woman he said, I will greatly multiply thy sorrow and thy conception; in sorrow thou shalt bring forth children; and thy desire shall be to thy husband, and he shall rule over thee.

17And unto Adam he said, Because thou hast hearkened unto the voice of thy wife, and hast eaten of the tree, of which I commanded thee, saying, Thou shalt not eat of it: cursed is the ground for thy sake; in sorrow shalt thou eat of it all the days of thy life;

18Thorns also and thistles shall it bring forth to thee; and thou shalt eat the herb of the field;

19In the sweat of thy face shalt thou eat bread, till thou return unto the ground; for out of it wast thou taken: for dust thou art, and unto dust shalt thou return.

20And Adam called his wife's name Eve; because she was the mother of all living.

21Unto Adam also and to his wife did the LORD God make coats of skins, and clothed them.

22And the LORD God said, Behold, the man is become as one of us, to know good and

evil: and now, lest he put forth his hand, and take also of the tree of life, and eat, and live

for ever:

23Therefore the LORD God sent him forth from the garden of Eden, to till the ground from

whence he was taken.

24So he drove out the man; and he placed at the east of the garden of Eden Cherubims,

and a flaming sword which turned every way, to keep the way of the tree of life.

So now we have Adam and Eve.

Chapter Seven

Cain, Able and the Others

And Adam knew Eve his wife; and she conceived, and bare Cain, and said, I have gotten a man from the LORD.

2And she again bare his brother Abel. And Abel was a keeper of sheep, but Cain was a tiller of the ground.

Cain was a tiller of the ground. So now we have a man to till the ground. We did not have one with Adam. Adam was presumably not a tiller of the ground. This signifies the need to sweat and toil and work the earth. The days of difficulty have befallen them.

3And in process of time it came to pass, that Cain brought of the fruit of the ground an offering unto the LORD.

4And Abel, he also brought of the firstlings of his flock and of the fat thereof. And the LORD had respect unto Abel and to his offering:

5But unto Cain and to his offering he had not respect. And Cain was very wroth, and his countenance fell.

6And the LORD said unto Cain, Why art thou wroth? and why is thy countenance fallen?

7If thou doest well, shalt thou not be accepted? and if thou doest not well, sin lieth at the door. And unto thee shall be his desire, and thou shalt rule over him.

8And Cain talked with Abel his brother: and it came to pass, when they were in the field, that Cain rose up against Abel his brother, and slew him.

9And the LORD said unto Cain, Where is Abel thy brother? And he said, I know not: Am I my brother's keeper?

10And he said, What hast thou done? the voice of thy brother's blood crieth unto me from the ground.

11And now art thou cursed from the earth, which hath opened her mouth to receive thy brother's blood from thy hand;

12When thou tillest the ground, it shall not henceforth yield unto thee her strength; a fugitive and a vagabond shalt thou be in the earth.

And so we have the first murder. But again it is stated *12When thou **tillest** the ground, it shall not henceforth yield unto thee her strength; a fugitive and a **vagabond** shalt thou be in the earth.*

Agriculture or "tilling" the earth was one of the few ways where people did not have to be nomadic. It is relatively new, about 6-10,000 years. So a little before Cains time but man is truly a vagabond without it. Without agriculture one has to be a hunter-gatherer, a nomad, a vagabond.

Now there is more evidence that Adam and Eve were not alone. *13And Cain said unto the LORD, My punishment is greater than I can bear.*
*14Behold, thou hast driven me out this day from the face of the earth; and from thy face shall I be hid; and I shall be a fugitive and a vagabond in the earth; and it shall come to pass, that **every one that findeth me shall slay me**.*

Everyone who? If Able is dead, isn't it just Cain and Adam and Eve? No. It clearly was not. Otherwise Cain would not have worried about it. He could easily avoid his parents…kids have been doing that since the beginning of time.

But it was the men and women from Genesis Chapter One that he was concerned about.

Chapter Eight

Cain's Wife

Further evidence of other people comes from the Land of Nod. *15And the LORD said unto him, Therefore* **whosoever** *slayeth Cain, vengeance shall be taken on him sevenfold. And the LORD set a mark upon Cain, lest any finding him should kill him. 16And Cain went out from the presence of the LORD, and dwelt in the land of Nod, on the east of Eden.*

17And Cain knew his wife; and she conceived, and bare Enoch: and he builded a city, and called the name of the city, after the name of his son, Enoch.

At this point one has to ask…why did Cain build a city? How many people would build a city for their wife and a single child? Its simple, you wouldn't. I assert there were in fact many people about. That assertion is born out by the further evidence that Lamech took wives which are not mentioned anywhere in the exhaustive genealogies that are written.

18And unto Enoch was born Irad: and Irad begat Mehujael: and Mehujael begat Methusael: and Methusael begat Lamech.

*19And Lamech took unto him **two wives**: the name of the one was **Adah, and the name of the other Zillah.***

So Lamech had two wives, in the Land of Nod. Where did they come from? And the previous passage also states *Therefore **whosoever** slayeth Cain*...Why would it say that unless there were other people?

It's at this point that the evidence becomes overwhelming, there were people everywhere. They are building cities, there are multiple wives. Cain is afraid that if he is marked any number of people might kill him. It seems evident that the 6,000-year question is irrelevant. Adam and Eve were most certainly not the first people.

The genealogy and lineage throughout the Bible is very concise...yet none of these wives are mentioned anywhere as having been born. But obviously they were born, just not unto the lineage of Adam and Eve. They were born unto the creation of God the Father (his part of the fence) prior to Adam and Eve.

The only reasonable conclusion is to take the Bible at face value, and it clearly states there were other people prior to Adam and Eve; the people of Genesis Chapter One.

Acknowledgements

I would of course like to thank God for being ever present in my life and helping to guide me steadily forward as I strive to understand this incredible universe in which we live. I am grateful to my children for bringing smiles to me every day and for giving me hugs and kisses in the sunshine and the rain.

I would like to thank my wife Shelly for her long lasting and steadfast support in the many endeavors that I routinely engage upon. I would like to give a very special thank you to all the people at AllAboutGOD.com Ministries for giving me permission to cite them; specifically Randall Niles for his patience in my incessant communication. I would also like to thank M. Houdmann and P. MATTHEWS-ROSE from the AllAboutGOD.com Ministries team. Many of the works cited in the "References" section were developed and edited by them and they have been kind enough to allow me to quote them. Their kindness however should not necessarily be interpreted as an endorsement of the material herein.

I would like to thank my parents, grandparents, aunts, uncles, cousins and brothers. Last but not least I would like to thank Amazon.com/Createspace and all of their team. Their kindness, dedication and acceptance of new ideas and authors has been of immeasurable worth and I am grateful to all of them.

The Art

The art is a collection of non-copyrighted images and has been certified as part of the public domain as follows.

The person or persons who have associated work with this document **meaning http://www.clker.com/** (the "Dedicator" or "Certifier") hereby either (a) certifies that, to the best of his knowledge, the work of authorship identified is in the public domain of the country from which the work is published, or (b) hereby dedicates whatever copyright the dedicators holds in the work of authorship identified below (the "Work") to the public domain. A certifier, moreover, dedicates any copyright interest he may have in the associated work, and for these purposes, is described as a "dedicator" below.

A certifier has taken reasonable steps to verify the copyright status of this work. Certifier recognizes that his good faith efforts may not shield him from liability if in fact the work certified is not in the public domain.

Dedicator makes this dedication for the benefit of the public at large and to the detriment of the Dedicator's heirs and successors. Dedicator intends this dedication to be an overt act of relinquishment in perpetuity of all present and future rights under copyright law, whether vested or contingent, in the Work. Dedicator understands that

such relinquishment of all rights includes the relinquishment of all rights to enforce (by lawsuit or otherwise) those copyrights in the Work.

Dedicator recognizes that, once placed in the public domain, the Work may be freely reproduced, distributed, transmitted, used, modified, built upon, or otherwise exploited by anyone for any purpose, commercial or non-commercial, and in any way, including by methods that have not yet been invented or conceived. The art was found solely at http://www.clker.com/ =-vector clip art online, royalty free and public domain.

References

The King James Version of the Bible was originally published in 1611.

Kaufmann, William J., III. Galaxies and Quasars. San Fransisco: W.H. Freeman and Company, 1979.

Silk, Joseph. A Short History of the Universe. New York: Scientific American Library, 1994.

Taylor, John. When the Clock Struck Zero. New York: St. Martins Press, 1993.

Trinh, Xuan Thuan. The Birth of the Universe: The Big Bang and After. New York: Harry N. Abrams, Inc., 1993.

Steven W. Hawking, George F.R. Ellis, "The Cosmic Black-Body Radiation and the Existence of Singularities in our Universe," *Astrophysical Journal,* 152, (1968) pp. 25-36.

Steven W. Hawking, Roger Penrose, "The Singularities of Gravitational Collapse and Cosmology," *Proceedings of the Royal Society of London,* series A, 314 (1970) pp. 529-548.

Mark Eastman, Chuck Missler, *The Creator: Beyond Time and Space,* (1996) p. 11.

W. Wayt Gibbs, "Profile: George F. R. Ellis," *Scientific American,* October 1995, Vol. 273, No.4, p. 55.

Richard Lewontin, "Billions and Billions of Demons," *New York Review of Books,* January 9, 1997, p. 28

Rasmussen, Ellis T. (1994) <u>Old Testament Commentary,</u> Deseret Book Co

World Wide Web

http://www.allaboutphilosophy.org/does-god-exist-c.htm

http://www.allabouttruth.org/holy-bible.htm

http://www.biblegateway.com/passage/?book_id=1&chapter=1&version=9

http://www.allaboutjesuschrist.org/is-jesus-god-c.htm

http://www.big-bang-theory.com/

See http://www.halos.com/reports/ext-2003-022.pdf

See http://www.halos.com/reports/arxiv-1998-rosetta.pdf and

http://www.halos.com/reports/ext-2003-021.pdf; see also

http://www.halos.com/reports/arxiv-1998-redshift.pdf and

http://www.halos.com/reports/arxiv-1998-affirmed.pdf

http://www.clker.com/

Personal Notes

Personal Notes

Made in the USA
Columbia, SC
15 November 2021

48999779R00037